HOW TO WRITE

How to start, and what to write if you don't
have any ideas

LOUISE TONDEUR

A Small Steps Guide

Welcome to How to Write

Why you should read this book

Hi. I'm Lou. I'm a writer and a writing tutor. I live on the sometimes sunny south coast of England. In this book, I offer you an alternative guide to starting to write.

If you're a total beginner, you're definitely in the right place. *How to Write* will also help if you've already done some writing but you need some writing exercises to inspire you.

I've been teaching Creative Writing for years and after a while it occurred to me that most writing books for beginners don't cover important tools like rhythm and sense of place. So I wrote some writing prompts, shared them with my students, who found them useful and different from the tools they had tried before. My list of writing prompts grew and grew over the years, and eventually turned into *How to Write*.

All the Small Steps Writing Guides in the series are based on two principles. One, you can take any big project, goal or task and break it down into smaller and smaller steps until it becomes doable. Two, if you take small but *specific* actions regularly enough, they'll have a snowball effect. That means, using the writing prompts in *How to Write*, you can take small steps towards achieving your writing goals.

A free course and help for beginners

You can find out more about my books and courses, including a free course for first time writers, by following the links from here: www.louisetondeur.co.uk and get advice and guidance on the writing life by following the links from my blog here: www.louisetondeur.co.uk/blog

Introduction

What's this book all about?

Over the course of the book you'll be introduced to seven writing techniques. By practising them, you'll become more confident at writing, and you'll develop your creative thinking by deliberately observing the world through each of the senses available to you.

I believe that you can learn a lot about writing through direct observation from life, like artists do. You're also going to learn how to give your reader an experience when they read your work, how to transport them into your writing, as it were, as if they were inside the story or poem having a look around.

You might have heard the advice to 'show not tell', which has become something of a writing cliché. (Don't worry, it's fine to 'tell' sometimes!) Through each of the sections of the book, you'll discover different ways to 'show not tell.'

So, this book covers seven different writing techniques:

- Limbering up
- Rhythm
- Sense of Place
- Word Pictures
- Objective Correlative
- Character
- Dialogue

Limbering up

The 'limbering up' exercises are designed to build your confidence and your creative thinking. You may wish to concentrate solely on these for a while if you have never written before and you need some gentle writing exercises to help you get going. You can also use them as warm ups at the start of a session or to generate ideas or to deepen your work on a particular character.

Rhythm

'Rhythm' is all about the rhythm and sound of language as well as the rhythms and sounds in everyday life, and of particular places. The way written language sounds (out loud or in our heads) is often neglected in favour of what we want to write about, whereas in everyday life we glean a lot of meaning from the way words are spoken. Learning about rhythm will mean your writing will create an experience for your readers from the start. It's also an innovative way to understand 'show not tell'.

Sense of place

'Sense of Place' is about observing the details of the places we inhabit, so we can use them in our writing. When we're writing creatively, we'll often need to associate a place with a character, and particularly with the way a character is feeling, using the objective correlative, which we'll discuss later on. It's possible to connect people and place, and to avoid unclear descriptions, by accessing each of the senses, using the practical activities in this section. Again, we're learning about showing verses telling.

Word pictures

'Word pictures' refer to the pictures you create on the page, and therefore in your readers' heads, or the pictures you create in your mind's eye, which you translate onto the page. It can also refer to images that use simile and metaphor, where you associate the thing you're describing with something else. In this section you'll learn how to create images in the mind's eyes and on the page. Like rhythm and sense of place, word pictures are another way to understand what 'showing' means.

Objective correlative

The 'objective correlative' involves describing an emotion or state of mind by transposing it onto an object, place or thing. Often when you're given the advice to 'show not tell' it means one of two things: 1) describe an event, as if it were unfolding in front of us, 2) use the objective correlative more effectively. Rhythm, sense of place and word pictures all help with the first of these. In this section we'll cover the second. You'll discover how to use the technique via practical activities, instead of reading the theory, but if you'd like to read T.S. Eliot's essay on the objective correlative, it's called 'Hamlet and His Problems' and it was published in 1921.

Character

'Character' involves creating people to populate your stories, as well as noticing the details of the people around you – these techniques can be incorporated into any kind of writing, including poetry and nonfiction. You'll use direct observation from life here, as you will all the way through the book, but you'll be noticing particular details about a person – a scar, the sound of their laugh, for instance – rather than trying to 'transcribe' whole person-alities. A character may be the first part of the story that you develop. Alternatively you can use the exercise to help you with an existing story.

Dialogue

'Dialogue' is about listening to people speak, and trying to reflect that when you write spoken word on the page. Learning about dialogue helps you to practise your listening skills and to translate your observations onto the page. Again, this isn't about transcribing actual conversa-tions, or trying to butt in on other people's business, but we are going to listen for interesting words and phrases that could inspire a story.

Each chapter is made up of six parts

To make this book easy to access, so you can find the tech-niques and tips that you need, each chapter is divided into the same six parts:

- Short Exercises
- Storytelling
- In your notebook

- Explore
- Extras
- and Design your own

Short exercises

These are designed to be done over a few minutes (depending on where they take you). Aim for 5 to 15 minutes per exercise.

Storytelling

You'll get storytelling tips, and discover ways to use the technique in question to create or begin a story. These exercises will help you to generate ideas for stories, or they will help you to structure an existing story.

In your notebook

While you may well want to do all of the activities in a notebook of course, these are research and gathering activities. You're treating your notebook as a place to collect material that you can use later.

Explore

You'll get a list of topics or techniques to research or explore on your own. Pick a couple. Use them to kick off an investigation into a particular subject or idea, or apply them to your writing to take it in a new direction.

Extras

Think of these are optional extras to use if you're particularly interested in the subject matter. They're techniques you can use to deepen your writing.

Design your own

I invite you to create your own DIY writing prompts as you go along, so that you have a set of powerful, tailor-made starting points to use later. If you find it useful, you can also spend more time observing something in particular (places or people for instance) to provide source material.

Prompts you design yourself are particularly powerful, because they are geared towards your own style of writing. You're going to look back over the writing prompts you've found particularly engaging and decide why, then use your observations to create your own versions.

Another key technique when creating your own prompts is to take your observations and the results of the writing activities in this book, and add 'what if?' Say you observed a man at a bus stop lighting a cigarette and throwing away the match. What if that match caught the near-by hedge alight? What if that is his last cigarette before X happens? What if the man falls asleep on the bus and X happens?

DIY writing prompts and resources

Creating your own prompts will mean this book will become a launch pad for your writing life. Your own prompts and observations will become more important to you than the starting points you'll find printed here. With this in mind, we'll come back to these 'DIY writing prompts' after you've worked through the book. I'll suggest other sources of writing prompts too.

In the resources section, I'll list suggested websites and the reading I've referred to throughout the book.

Why do these activities?

Mainly, these activities are designed to build your confidence and to help you let go of the judgement and self-criticism that so often goes along with creative work, and to get some words down. That way you'll get over your fear of the blank page and collect source material for yourself so you can play with it later.

Not all of the activities will be useful or will chime with you, although often the exercises outside your comfort zone end up being the ones you really need to do. Once you've done the activities, the secret is in the redrafting. If you like, you can come back and mine the short pieces of writing you've created in response to these activities in order to create something longer or more finished.

For example, you might end up with a story idea, a bunch of characters you like, a dialogue you want to use, the start of a poem, a treatment for a screenplay or stage play, or some ideas for blog posts or feature articles. Most of all, I hope you end up with a regular writing habit. That doesn't have to be every day, it simply needs to be regular.

1

Limbering up

An introduction to limbering up

This section is all about how to get started. Just as limbering up helps you to prepare for a work out, these activities help you to prepare for writing. So you might use them at the beginning of a session. Alternatively, if you haven't written before, dive into the limbering up exercises as a way of getting your writing habit off the ground.

Creative thinking might involve connecting concepts or things that aren't usually connected (an umbrella and a brick, for instance), it might also involve novelty of some other kind, the umbrella shop where you move a few bricks at the back and discover... Both of those things – unusual connections and novelty – take confidence and we also need to learn to bypass the internal censor or judge that tells us not to be 'silly'. All of the prompts in this book are designed to help you to develop confidence and to think creatively. These limbering up activities are particularly good for getting round the internal censor or judge that tells you your writing isn't good enough, the first step towards greater confidence and creativity.

I mentioned a writing habit. If you're only writing sporadically at the moment, or as the mood takes you, then you can use these activities to encourage yourself to write regularly.

Find a time and space to write and come up with a shorthand for the activities you find most useful. (For instance FW for freewriting, or a quick doodle of a car for familiar journeys, or of a book for book mining. You'll find out more below.) Go through your diary or calendar adding in shorthand for the activity whenever you plan to write. Do five minutes to start with until you've built up to twenty-five minute blocks. Later on you can join twenty-five minute blocks together to create longer writing sessions.

Limbering up: short exercises

Freewriting. This is a well-known writing technique, that goes by different names. I think the term freewriting first turned up in Peter Elbow's book called *Writing with Power*. It sometimes gets called 'stream of consciousness writing'. If you've read Creative Writing books or been on courses before, you've probably come across this technique, but if not it can be pretty mind-blowing first time you try it! Not everyone loves freewriting, but give it a try and find out if it works for you.

Put all of the rules away. Don't worry about spelling, punctuation or grammar, or even about keeping your words on the line if you're writing freehand. You don't have to make sense or write anything interesting. You could even repeat the same word over and over, or write lists.

The only thing you must do is keep going. Use a timer.

If you've never done this before, start with a minute. Otherwise, go for five minutes. You can simply write what's in your head, or you can start with a prompt word like 'blue' or 'the sea'. You can also start by using the senses; write down what you can hear for one minute, for example.

Try some freewriting over the next week. See if you can build up your time from one minute to five minutes or from five minutes to ten minutes. If you're already an expert, try half an hour.

Book mining. Create a pile of at least ten books. Go to the library to do this if you like. Take a word from the middle of page 8, 32, 64 and 102 in each book. Pick nouns or verbs. Do this a few times on different days, using different books. Keep the list of words in your notebook. Write sentences that include these words. Circle three words. Have two people talking and have them mention these three words. Write a scene where someone walks to work. Have them see or do some of the things on your list on the way.

Familiar journeys. Take three familiar journeys that you go on regularly. If you would usually drive, either find an alternative way to travel so you can write, or recall the journey at the end of the day and write what you remember. These don't have to be remarkable journeys – ordinary is fine. For example, I get the bus to the swimming pool; I used to walk through the cemetery to my yoga class; I take the train to visit my mum. Next time you do these journeys, take a notebook with you and pause three times along the route. Simply write a list of the things you can see, hear, taste, touch, smell and sense. You could also design your own five to fifteen minute writing walks around your local area. As with the book mining, play around with the words, experimenting with them in sentences.

Limbering up: storytelling

You created a fair amount of source material during the first set of limbering up exercises. Work with it to create these stories. You might end up with a set of story ideas, or the beginning to several stories, or the outline to one story. Take this in any direction you like.

Circle the words and phrases you like from the freewriting, book mining, and familiar journeys exercises. Imagine two people. Give them some of the words and phrases that came up in the short exercises. Play around with this – they don't have to speak the words. For instance, if you noticed bright green leaves during one of your journeys, then you could give them one of a bright green T-shirt.

What if? Using the words and phrases you like from the short exercises, add the phrase 'what if?' and see where it takes you. By the way, it was Stanislavski who wrote about the magic of the phase 'what if?' on the stage, in a book called *An Actor Prepares*. Sometimes it's known as 'the magic if'. As we saw earlier, 'What if?' involves using your imagination to push a starting point a bit further, and then further still. For example, say you observed rubbish on the street as you walked to the gym. What if the refuse collectors went on long term strike? What would happen? Or what if, sometimes in the future, we lived in a world where the rubbish was never collected? Say a fallen tree came up for you when you were freewriting. How might you apply 'what if?' and then push it a little further still?

Limbering up: in your notebook

Make a note of the exercises you've done so far and the effect they've had on you. Did they make you excited, peaceful, tired, interested, uncomfortable, curious, happy, unhappy, bored, uneasy, fascinated? Write down how you responded. Different exercises will work for different people. Aim to repeat those that made you feel happy, excited or curious, or that made you see the world slightly differently. Uncomfortable can be good too, but stay just outside your comfort zone, not way outside it.

Over a week make a note of the times you have most energy, and the times you have the least energy.

Make a note of the times when you could fit in a fifteen minute writing session. Couple this with *where* you'll write – say over lunch, or on the train home.

Of everything you've done so far, do any themes emerge? Is there anything you want to explore further? Circle it or underline it.

Limbering up: explore

Art galleries,
beaches,
cartoons,
familiar places,
junk shops,
landmarks,
libraries,
local museums,
old buildings,
photos,
postcards,
walks.

Limbering up: extras

Go to the library and find the section on Creative Writing. Make a pile of books. Do the book mining exercise again, but adapt it as follows. Flick through each one. Does it contain any short exercises (often in bullet points at the end of chapters) or any writing prompts? If they're not obvious, try the contents page, but don't spend too long on each book.

Note the title and author of each book so you could find it again. Using a list format, get down the essential information about each writing exercise or prompt – i.e. there's no need to copy it out in full, simply make notes. Add these to your repertoire.

Limbering up: design your own

This is where you get a chance to design your own writing prompts to use later. As we're simply starting out in this section, we'll get into the detail in the next section. For now, take another look at what you've done so far. In particular, re-read the words and phrases you've collected. Could you make up some 'rules' for yourself that include some of these words and phrases? Come up with at least six of these and have fun with it!

For example, if the phrase you like is 'fallen tree', your prompt could be: write about a street where a tree falls across the road in the middle of the night. Or if your phrase was 'noisy traffic', your prompt could be: write a poem using other words beginning with n and t.

2

Rhythm

An introduction to rhythm

It can be tempting to start with content, or what you want to write about, the theme, idea, person or place or story you want to describe or investigate, and then to get stuck because you don't know how to make progress. As an antidote to that, now we've limbered up, we're starting with rhythm.

Rhythm and the next section, on sense of place, will both help you to keep going when you're overwhelmed and don't know what to write next.

We're also focusing on rhythm from the get go, because the way language sounds when it's read often gets forgotten. Short sentences are snappy. Longer sentences meander leisurely and can have a calming, soporific effect on the reader.

Sentence length is only one aspect to consider. Tone, the sounds in an environment, onomatopoeic words and the weight of words in your mouth all have an impact. Rhythm is a skill poets in particular may want to focus on, but the techniques discussed in this section are for all kinds of writers.

Life has a backing track, with a rhythm to it. Standing in a forest feels very different to standing in a supermarket, partly because of continually repeated sounds that have a particular cadence and tone. If we can communicate this to a reader, we'll help to transport them into our poems and stories in their imaginations.

Everyday life has a rhythm to it too, in that our daily, weekly, monthly and yearly routines punctuate our existence. People in stories participate in these 'rhythms of life', or 'life routines,' to put it more mundanely.

As writers we experience these rhythms and they affect our ability to turn up and write as much as they affect the content of our stories.

Rhythm: short exercises

Use these rhythms to inspire your writing or try to replicate them as you write.

- Find a clock that ticks loudly as you write.
- Write on a train or imagine writing on a train.
- Listen to the rhythm of your own heartbeat with your eyes closed. Clear your head. What images come to mind?
- Imagine a heartbeat as you write.
- Next time it rains, go and write next to a window.
- Events have rhythms: a picnic, a breakfast, an argument, a walk, a swim, a phone conversation, cleaning the house. Pick one to describe.

Rhythm: storytelling

In these stories, concentrate on how the words sound rather than on what happens in the story.

Try writing down your thoughts for a minute, then build to five minutes, then ten. Read out loud and listen to the pattern and rhythm of your own thoughts.

Create the sound of footsteps or a baby crying or a wheel squeaking using written words. Come back to this later – does it sound like the start of a story?

Create a story that includes a series of rhythms that start off slowly and quietly, build up to make lots of noise and then die down again. Situate your story somewhere first.

For instance, a supermarket could have a trolley with a squeaky wheel, a baby crying, a till beeping, background music and a customer announcement.

Rhythm: in your notebook

Collect sounds by visiting interesting (rhythmic) places and writing while you are there. Try a supermarket, a tube station, a field, or a museum.

Collect rhythmic or onomatopoeic or interesting-sounding words and phrases in a notebook. Chop them up and move them around to make a poem.

Collect other sound words: rhythm, speak, volume, rattle, for example.

Collect other words in categories. Make lists. For example, weather words: ice, snow, hail, sunshine, thunder, or city words: bus, roadworks, pavements, offices, litter.

Use the sound words and word categories to experiment with the sounds of words and word combinations

without worrying about sense. Use punctuation and
different sentence lengths to change the rhythm of what
you write.

Rhythm: explore

Alliteration,
beat boxes,
bouncing,
broken sentences,
clocks,
dancing,
dashes,
echoes,
falling,
fighting,
footsteps,
journeys,
musical notes,
patterns,
repetition,
syntax,
ringing,
sea,
seasons,
singing,
sirens,
trains,
voices,
witches.

Rhythm: extras

Collect examples words that conform to different rhythms in your notebook:

- Iamb. Unstress / stress. Example: Compare.
- Trochee. Stress / unstress. Example: Trochee.
- Spondee. Stress / stress. Example: Batman.
- Look up the rules for writing a villanelle, a sonnet and a Haiku. This website has a description of poetic forms: www.poets.org/poetsorg/collection/poetic-forms

Rhythm: design your own

Spend a day looking out for rhythms. Carry your notebook with you to jot them down or record what you discover at the end of the day. These could be rhythms you particularly like or jarring rhythms that annoy you. In fact, if you can pair an emotion to the rhythms you discover, so much the better.

Make a list of the rhythms you discover and turn them into writing prompts to use later.

Add 'what if?' to your observations. Say you observed birds singing, the gush of water running over rocks, the sound of a helicopter, the beeping traffic, a chainsaw. Add a bit of imagination using 'what if?', like this: What if a man were blindfold and could only hear birds singing, the gush of water nearby, and the sound of a helicopter overhead? What if a couple were caught in a traffic jam full of beeping traffic on their way to a wedding / to rob a bank / to get to a dying relative / to enter a surfing competition? What if the bird song were interrupted by the sound of a chainsaw? For instance, you might end up writing a story that includes the sound of bird song and the sound of a helicopter and the journey to see the dying relative, or a poem that involves a chainsaw and the sound of running water.

3

Sense of place

An introduction to sense of place

Writing always involves place. We write in particular places. We write about specific places. We set our stories on location. We evoke places in our poems. We remember pertinent places from our childhoods and write about them.

Even writing about nowhere, or about an absence of location, or a longing for somewhere to call home, is about place in a visceral as well as a cerebral way. This will connect with what you learn about the objective correlative later.

So place will affect our writing lives over and over again. The best way to understand place is to go out and experience it, and the best way to record that experience is through the senses. If you can't go out, use the place where you are.

We can avoid a vague, generalised descriptions of place by deliberately going through each of the senses available to us one after another and listing what we experience. You can mine that information during future writing projects to help you to describe places.

This section introduces you to writing about place. Why does it come before character? And why haven't I included a section on 'plotting' or 'narrative structure' or 'poetic form' when I have included a section on place? Because there are plenty of resources out there on plotting and structure. K.M. Weiland's books are good if you need a guide, for instance, and so is Lisa Cron's work.

Although place affects not only how we write and what we write about but also where we write, it often gets neglected in books for beginner writers. Here I'm inviting you to learn about sense of place from the start of your writing journey.

Sense of place: short exercises

Describe a person in a place using one of the following:

- a castle,
- a school,
- a garden,
- a city square,
- a sitting room,
- a waiting room,
- a train station.

Now try these prompts:

- Describe a library from the point of view of a homeless person.
- Describe an island from the point of view of a seagull.

- Describe somewhere frightening or somewhere comforting.
- Invent a place. Describe it. Now give it a personality.
- Use a place to convey emotion. Make a place angry, sad, disappointed, happy, surprised or delighted.

Sense of place: storytelling

Think of a place that you know well, but not somewhere you have lived. Describe it.

Invent a fictional character to go with it. Write a poem or a story from the point of view of that character.

Imagine a place that is haunted. Write about the things or people that haunt it.

Create a made up character. Decide on a specific place for them to exist. Describe how they feel about the place. Write a monologue or a dialogue.

Think of a place that you know well. Imagine the people who may have lived there and the memories that the place holds. Give the place an atmosphere.

Sense of place: in your notebook

- Collect places and spaces in your notebook. Put yourself in interesting places and describe them briefly.
- Collect emotions in your notebook. Make a list.
- Spend time matching emotions to places. The lonely wall, the angry sitting room, the mournful library.

- Collect elements of places or atmospheres in your notebook. For example, the texture of a wall, the changing weather, the interplay of sunshine and shadows, the twists and turns of the undergrowth.
- Watch a place over a year. Observe how it changes with the seasons. Write about how it feels to be there.

Sense of place: explore

Architecture,
beaches,
broken down buildings,
close description,
creating atmospheres,
deserts,
emotions and places,
forests,
geography,
headlands,
homes,
inhospitable places,
identity,
islands,
memory and history,
murderous places,
nowhere,
ordinary places,
passing of time,
personification,
quiet places,
restricted areas,

seasons,
space,
strange places,
terraforming,
unnerving places,
welcoming / unwelcoming places.

Sense of place: extras

Jot down some ideas for a short film. Use elements of the environment to create either a sense of happiness or a sense of unease. For example, set the film in one room. Describe the light through the window, the stains on the floor, the texture of the walls.

Go and sit in a place with your notebook and write what you observe. As you write, try to link a particular emotion to the elements of the place you are writing about. Try not to mention the emotion – try to make your reader feel the emotion.

Sense of place: design your own

Spend a day observing the places around you. As before, take your notebook with you or reflect on your discoveries at the end of the day. These might be places you pass, inhabit or otherwise interact with every day, or you could go out of your way to investigate interesting places on the day you choose.

Make a list of the places you observe and turn them into writing prompts to use later. Here's one way of doing that:

Use your observations to suggest a character or characters in a place. For example, if one of your places was a supermarket, you could create a fictional supermarket worker who has to do extra shifts to make ends meet. That character becomes a writing prompt when you add 'what if?' By the way, the work you did on rhythm would also come into play if you're writing about a supermarket: the checkouts, the customer service announcements and tinny music would punctuate your character's day.

4

Word pictures

An introduction to word pictures

You've already discovered rhythm and sense of place, so you're getting used to involving your senses and your observations of the world around you when you write. In this section, you're going to use some of the skills you've already learnt to play around with language.

Our adult selves can be suspicious of 'play' and 'games' because they seem childish. Part of the life of a writer is about learning to structure a poem or story or play, and part of it is about learning to market and sell your work if that's what you want to do, both 'adult' skills if you like. However, we mustn't forget creative thinking, which translates into creative practice, or playing with words on the page.

Creative visualisation means picturing a scene or a person in your head in detail before writing about them – and creating a 'word picture' from the picture in your imagination. If you're a visual thinker, it can help to visualise a scene in detail before writing about it.

I invite you to play for the sake of playing and to have fun with word games but for those who need it there are at least two serious reasons behind this section on word pictures. Firstly, this book is all about building your confidence as you think creatively about your work. Playing with words allows you to do just that. Secondly, this section will help you to create pictures in your readers' minds.

Not everyone can think visually, but most people can; learning how to create word pictures will enhance the experience of these readers, and will increase clarity and understanding for all your readers, and as a result they're much more likely to keep reading.

Word pictures: short exercises

There's no right or wrong way to create your word pictures but here are some top tips: employ detail and specificity, and observation from real life using the senses. What can you see? What can you hear? What can you taste? What can you touch? What can you smell? What can you sense? Right now, write down one line for each of these sensations.

During the following, attempt to create a word picture in the reader's head using more than one of your senses:

- Think about a recent journey. Describe the colours you saw using word pictures.
- Create lists of nouns. Turn each one into a word picture.
- What is it like to wait and wait for something? Describe the feeling using word pictures.
- Write about the sea. Describe a photograph. Describe a stone.

- Write about a desert by answering this question: what is it like to be very thirsty?

Word pictures: storytelling

When creating the following, concentrate on creating unusual word pictures rather than on what happens in the story.

- Try freewriting for five minutes. Focus on your senses. Do another five minutes. This time focus on colours. Later, redraft what you wrote, using word pictures.
- Sit and watch an object for five minutes. Now describe it. Later, redraft answering the question: What did the object remind me of? Repeat this using different locations.
- Sit somewhere you don't usually write. Write a description using each of the senses. Later, redraft what you wrote and create an unusual or strange description of each of these sensory experiences.
- Describe a giant. Create a picture of the giant in the reader's head. Use descriptions or pictures of other concrete things to create a feeling of what the giant is like. E.g. he had fists like sheep and legs like ladders. And, using 'what if?', decide what happens to the giant when he tries to make friends. If you like, create the start of a children's story called 'The Giant'.

Word pictures: in your notebook

- Collect lists of interesting things you see during your day.
- Write a random list of things: House, tree, witch, stick, ball etc.
- Write a second list: Pencil, book, fire, mouse, present etc.
- Just for fun, make pairs of words, taking one word from each list: house book, tree fire, witch pencil, stick mouse, ball present.
- Create sentences using one word to describe the other. The house opened up like a book. The tree had leaves the colour of fire. Play around with the order of the words in the sentences you have created.
- Pick a sentence that you like from the results and describe an object using word pictures.
- Make the ordinary unordinary. Using unusual pairings of words, create a picture that will make the reader think, or see things from a new angle.

Word pictures: explore

Arguments,
blindness,
close description,
the colour of conversations,
colours,
danger,
death and rebirth,
defamiliarisation,

dragons,
emotions,
feelings,
Greek myths,
houses,
invisibility,
magic,
metaphor,
mourning,
movement,
nature,
ordinariness,
people,
pictures,
sea,
seasons,
senses,
simile,
tempestuousness,
wakefulness,
zaniness.

Word pictures: extras

- Metaphor: a phrase or word that is not literally true but is used to describe something else. The lake was a mirror, for example.
- Metonym: where something related to the thing is used to stand in for it. The Lions, for instance, is used to refer to the England football team, because of the three lions logo on their shirts.

- Synecdoche: a type of metonym, where a part represents the whole. The crown is used to mean the royal family, for instance.
- Tip: Metonymy and synecdoche are frequently used on TV and in sports commentary. Make a list of examples then use one to kickstart a story.

Word pictures: design your own

As before, spend a day observing different places and people. Carry your notebook with you or record your observations at the end of the day. No judgement – simply be curious. Turn this into a list of words and phrases. Add some emotions to your list – pair emotion words with your observations at random.

Take your list of words and phrases and turn them into writing prompts to use later. You could link contrasting observations together, and make yourself a 'writing rule' or constraint. So for instance, write a story or a poem that must include two of the pairs of words you came up with and where the ordinary must become unordinary somehow.

5

Objective correlative

An introduction to the objective correlative

Made famous by T.S. Eliot, the objective correlative involves linking an emotion with an object or place or thing.

Let's take an object – a wall, for instance. A wall doesn't have any intrinsic emotion attached to it, it's just a stack of bricks held together somehow, probably by cement, but we're so used attributing meaning to the thing we've called 'a wall' that it's actually hard to think of one without an emotion attached.

Let's think about another 'thing' that's often associated with emotion: a ray of sunlight. The process of photons traveling from the surface to the sun to the earth doesn't have any intrinsic emotion attached, but if you read about a ray of light in a story it would provide a shortcut to a particular emotion (hope), although rather a clichéd one. Anytime you evoke an emotion using an object, place or thing, you've used the objective correlative. Try to do it in a new way. Avoid rays of sunlight.

Using the objective correlative (or linking an emotion to an object or place or thing) is so much more powerful than simply telling us about how you feel or how a fictional character feels. Consider the difference between 'Jo stood on the beach feeling happy' and 'Jo stood on the sand, tiny waves tickling her feet, the sun warming her face'.

You can also link the emotion to actions or behaviours. Consider the difference between 'John felt angry' and 'John threw the chrysanthemum down on the path in front of him and stamped on it'.

Objective correlative: short exercises

Make a list of ordinary household objects, such as kettle, picture frame, television, cushion. You can do this by looking around your own environment. Write two or three sentences describing a character feeling lonely, nostalgic, happy or sad. Don't mention the emotion but have them interact with the objects on your list.

Go outside or look outside and do something similar. Make a list of objects outside, like this: tree, hosepipe, trowel, plant pot, trug, paving stone. You might also note down what the weather is doing today and colours that you see. Again, write two or three sentences describing a character feeling lonely, nostalgic, happy or sad. Pick a different emotion this time. Don't mention the emotion but describe the objects, weather, or colours.

Use the elements of earth, water, air and fire as headings in a notebook and jot down words and phrases associated with them. These might be things or situations that use earth, water, air, and fire, like helicopter, tractor, forge or boat, or they could be looser associations like fairy, plants, bonfire night or shark. Get down as many as you can in 5 minutes.

Take the same elements – earth, water, air and fire – and write down any emotions or states of mind that you might associate with each. There's no right or wrong answer, simply jot down whatever comes to mind. For example, flighty, scatty, untidy for air, or down-to-earth, down in the dumps, reliable, for earth.

Here's the difficult part. Take your two lists: words and phrases associated with earth, water, air and fire and your list of emotions and states of mind and combine them. Start with your favourite. For example, pick one 'thing' about earth and one earth-like emotion or state of mind. Write about the emotion by describing the thing. Keep going for five minutes.

Sit somewhere quiet, preferably somewhere you can observe nature, but a café or train station could also work. Watch what's going on around you. Note down (quickly) how you are feeling. Observe again for a couple of minutes. Again, note down (quickly) how you are feeling. Repeat this a few times. Did the emotion change? Did what you were watching affect how you were feeling? Did your emotion colour what you were watching?

Describe a character sitting in a park, in a café or a train station. It may help to think about what's just happened to them, in the previous 'scene' as it were. You're looking through his or her eyes, experiencing the world through his or her senses. What can he or she see, hear, touch, taste and smell? Experience the world through his or her emotions and point of view. Imagining that you are this person, write a description of what you can see. Without mentioning any emotional states, convey how this character is feeling.

Objective correlative: storytelling

The short exercises you've had a go at so far in this chapter will have given you some material, ideas for characters, descriptions, perhaps the beginning of something. Develop these into a list of story ideas or one story outline. Focus particularly on the characters.

Circle the words and phrases you like from short exercises you've done so far. Now imagine a location in detail and write for twenty-five minutes, making use of these words and phrases. Play around and see what happens.

For instance, perhaps you wrote about a wistful character watching a bonfire when you did the earth, air, fire and water exercise. Describe the rest of the environment. Perhaps you thought of a grief-stricken character on a park bench for the last of the short exercises. Fill in the rest of the details. Use this location to start a story.

What if? Using the words and phrases you highlighted, add 'what if?' and see where it takes you. For instance, imagine a lonely character trudging around a paved garden holding a trowel and a plant pot, where there's a tree, a hosepipe, and trug full of flowers. What if...? Fill in the gaps.

Describe the character and what happens next. Convey the sense of loneliness without mentioning any emotion words. Alternatively, you could have two characters meet – the wistful bonfire watcher and the grief-stricken park dweller, for example – what if they met and...?

Joined up thinking. Take aspects you like from several of the short exercises and the storytelling exercises you've done so far and work out (make up) the connections between them. They can be as wacky as you like, because you don't have to show anyone.

Top tip: giving characters a specific job (in the loosest

sense of that word) and being specific about his or her location can help you make them authentic. Specificity is key.

Objective correlative: in your notebook

Carry your notebook with you and make a note of interesting places, objects, things, colours, weather, ephemera, rubbish blowing along the street.

You might also like to note down your experience of these things using your senses. What did the litter sound like as it blew along the street? What did the weather feel like on your skin? What did the rain taste like? How did the place smell? Did it remind you of a smell you've experienced before, or a combination of smells? Did the colours make you think of something else of a similar colour or conjure up an emotion for you?

When you get a quiet moment, sit down and contemplate your list. Add emotions or mental states and experiment with phrases. These don't have to make sense. Angry litter, embarrassed pink door, proud train ticket. This gets you to think about how things can convey emotion; simply save the words and phrases you come up with and look at them later. They may well kick off an idea for a piece of writing, a story or a character or help you to describe a place in an interesting way.

Objective correlative: explore

Breeze,
cafés
emotion or feeling words,
farms,

fire-states, and different uses of fire,
flight,
forests,
made-made open spaces,
marine environments,
movement,
objects,
the senses,
smoke and steam and things that produce it,
states of mind,
train stations,
watery environments,
weather events.

Objective correlative: extras

Watch 3 or 4 films or TV shows over the next few weeks and look out for times where they associate an object, place or thing with an emotion or state of mind. Record instances of the objective correlative in your notebook and make a note of which film or TV show it came from.

Read a chapter from your favourite novel or a page from one of your favourite short stories and look to see if the author has linked an object, place or thing with an emotion or state of mind. How often do they do it? Are they rather over-used instances of the objective correlative, like the ray of sunlight? Or are they highly inventive and unusual?

How does the use of the objective correlative affect how much you enjoy the story? 'The Swimmer' by John Cheever (a short story published in the New Yorker in 1964) is a good example if you need one.

Objective correlative: design your own

Spend a day (or even a week) collecting emotions and states of mind. Carry your notebook with you or record your observations at the end of the day. Note down the ways in which these emotions and states of mind are expressed.

Are there particular gestures, movements, body language or facial expressions involved? Some people express emotions more openly than others of course, but there are often subtle 'tells'. And how do you experience emotion in your body? Where do you feel it and what does it feel like?

Admittedly, it can be difficult to take a step back when you're in the midst of an emotion or watching someone go through a particular emotion. Mindfulness techniques are wonderful for this. Dinty Moore's book *The Mindful Writer* may help if you wish to learn more about mindfulness and writing.

Alternatively, you can perform the same 'observations' of emotions and states of mind by looking back and remembering times in the past when you experienced certain emotional states and making notes. Balance this out by remembering happy times as well as difficult ones.

A quick reminder

You can find out more about my books and courses, including a free course for first time writers, by following the links from here: www.louisetondeur.co.uk and get advice and guidance on the writing life by following the links from my blog here: www.louisetondeur.co.uk/blog

6

Character

An introduction to character

Made-up people populate stories of all kinds; you might also write about real life people and need to render them using specific detail so your reader understands them. Poems, too, can be based on observations of people and behaviour and often involve a fictional 'lyric I', the imagined person who is 'speaking' the poem.

We've already started to create characters. Now we're going deeper. How do you translate people so that they appear on the page and come to life in our readers' imaginations? How do you use observations of people – strangers, friends, family, remembered people, historical and contemporary figures – to make your writing stronger? That's what this section is all about.

We've been dealing with characters in the previous sections and that's important because the skills you've already developed will help you to create people who seem to live and breathe and have a life of their own off the page. In this section you'll build on the work you've already done and use your powers of observation to think more specifically about characterisation and 'people creation'.

Before we start, I'll say a quick word about point of view. Point of view, in this context, means seeing the world through the eyes of a character or narrator or speaker. This could be an actual person if you're writing nonfiction. Think of it as a pair of tinted glasses, if you like, a particular way of seeing the world.

You might wonder why I've only covered point of view in passing in this book. Shouldn't it have its own section? Through all of the work you're doing on character (including the exercises in this section) you've automatically been honing your 'point of view' skills. Take any of these character activities further and write for extended periods, and you'll be practising point of view too.

Character: short exercises

- As you go about your everyday life, observe people on trains, at work, in cafés, in the street.
- Try freewriting: write as if you were a fictional character for five minutes.
- Make a list of jobs. Make a list of locations. Now write a description of a fictional character with that job, in that place.
- Write a purely physical description of a fictional character. Write a purely emotional description of a fictional character. Use images. Combine the two descriptions to make one person.
- Write about two opposites. Pick any you like. Hot and cold, land and sea etc. Use these notes to describe two characters.

Character: storytelling

Make up a character based on the people you observed or the other exercises you've done so far.

Give your character a quirk, unusual hobby, intriguing habit, gesture or physical tick, or a special interest that requires clothes or equipment. This character is on a train.

Now describe the way their skin feels and the way their hair is shaped, the way they smile. Write down what's going on in the mind of your character. Write down a description of the way someone else views the same character.

Invent three or four characters this way. Put all of your characters on the train. Describe what each is doing on the train, who is sitting next to whom, where they are going, and whether they are good travellers or not.

- Two of these characters talk to one another.
- Something happens on the train, a small event that gets a reaction. Write about it.
- Another small event occurs, caused by one of the characters. Write about what happens next.

Character: in your notebook

- Collect fictional characters either by visiting interesting places or as you go about your day-to-day life. Who might inhabit the café, the park, the art gallery, the cathedral, the beach?
- Collect character trait words: vain, religious, clumsy, lonely, magical.
- Collect jobs. A job is a great way into character creation.

- Collect locations. If you put particular person, in a particular job, in a particular place, you've started a story.
- Collect ephemera. Make lists or create a scrapbook. Collect the minutia of a character's day. Use your ephemera for a poem or flash fiction or to start a screenplay.

Character: explore

Alienation,
background research,
body language,
buildings,
changing emotions,
close descriptive writing,
conversations,
crowds,
cultures,
environments,
faces,
images,
jobs,
loneliness,
meetings,
metaphor,
movement,
objective correlative,
old age,
personification,
places,
possessions,
relationships,

touch,
unspoken dialogue,
verisimilitude.

Character: extras

Here are some well-known fictional characters. Create
scenarios where two of these characters meet each other.

- Fitzwilliam Darcy (from Jane Austen's *Pride and Prejudice*)
- Ford Prefect (from Douglas Adams' 'Hitchhiker's Guide' series)
- The Governess (from Henry James's *The Turn of the Screw*)
- Hamm (from Beckett's *Endgame*)
- Jane Eyre (from the novel of the same name by Charlotte Brontë)
- Mrs. Malaprop (from *The Rivals* by Richard Sheridan)
- Sherlock Holmes (the famous detective invented by Arthur Conan Doyle)
- Viola (from Shakespeare's *Twelfth Night*)

Character: design your own

Spend a day observing the people around you. As before,
take your notebook with you or reflect the different characters you observed at the end of the day. Note down particular details that you notice, rather than 'whole' people. A
scar across the cheek, the way their eyes smile, the way
they push their glasses up their nose, or stand with their
weight on one leg.

Do it this way because making notes on 'whole' people

is impossible: you probably only know one or two sides of the people you interact with daily, or know them so well it will prove hard to take notes. Instead of using well-worn phrases, like smiling through the pain, for instance, focus on the detail of the observation, like three tiny folds at the side of each eye.

Make a spark box. Get an old tissue box (because they have a ready-made hole in the top). Cut up some slips of paper. On each slip of paper, write a different idea. This can be a word, phrase, character, sound or place. The idea is that you stick your hand into the spark box and pull out a 'spark' that you then use in a piece of writing. You can decide on the rule in advance (the 'spark' must appear in the opening line, for instance) or leave it open.

For example, you could write the rhythms you collected earlier onto your pieces of paper and put them in your 'spark' box. If you leave them there long enough they may even take you by surprise when you pull one out!

In this instance, create a character-based spark box. Fill it with possible jobs, quirks, deepest desires, secrets, motivations or lines of dialogue.

7

Dialogue

An introduction to dialogue

This section on dialogue goes hand in hand with the last one on character. Getting peoples' voices right is important from the point of view of believability and authenticity. This is harder than it seems. Simply transcribe a 'real' conversation and it won't sound like polished written dialogue. People repeat themselves, don't say what they mean, don't speak in whole sentences, go round the houses, and use idioms and clichés.

As well as all that, much of the 'message' of what we say comes from body language, gestures and inflection, and has little to do with the meaning of the words. Think of the number of different ways in which you can say 'ok' or 'thanks', for example. If that aspect is missed in the written word, the reader will experience it as inauthentic (and may not know why).

Therefore, written dialogue has to reflect that and still be clear enough for the reader to understand. It's a balancing act. In traditionally written prose, dialogue has to sound like 'real' speech but has to be contrived enough to be clear, without us noticing the contrivance.

As you'll find out when you work through this section, dialogue is affected by context, particularly place and the status of a character, social or otherwise. Observation of dialogue (deliberately listening in) helps you to get your characters' voices right but don't try to write it down verbatim. Have a go at the following exercises and you'll see what I mean.

Dialogue: short exercises

Watch people around you. Listen to the way they speak and interact. Use your observation as inspiration in these short exercises.

Write a dialogue that happens in one of the following places:

- On a train
- At a school
- At a crematorium
- At a fun fair
- On a boat

Create a conversation where:

- the people speak in one or two word sentences.
- the people only speak in clichés.
- the people communicate through body language more than words.

Dialogue: storytelling

Use these conversations to tell a story and to establish your characters:

- Write a conversation where the speakers are not named. Establish who is speaking through the sound of their voice and what they say, their body language and their attitudes.
- Write a conversation where the people involved don't say what they really think or feel. Imply this in the language you use and the voice of the narrator.
- Write a close description of an imaginary scene set in either a forest, a temple, or a seascape. Now create two characters and place them in the scene. Let them have a conversation.

Dialogue: in your notebook

Put yourself in situations where you can overhear people speaking. (Be subtle and keep yourself safe while you do this!) Write in / on:

- galleries and museums,
- cafés
- buses,
- trains,
- other public places.

Collect overheard lines of dialogue. Listen to people's conversations and the way they use language. Listen to the pattern of the voices. Try to capture these patterns in your notebook later on, but don't try to transcribe whole conversations.

Take a phrase that you have heard. Invent the rest of the conversation.

Watch how people communicate. Observe their body language. Make a note of facial expressions, eye movements, gestures, whether movements are open or closed, friendly or hostile.

Dialogue: explore

Arguments,
body language,
broken or unfinished sentences,
interruptions,
clichés,
communication / lack of communication,
facial expressions,
feelings,
overlaps,
pauses,
relationships,
shouting,
silence,
subtext,
telephone conversations,
thoughts,
voices,
whispering.

Dialogue: extras

- Write a conversation in prose as if you're writing a short story and punctuate it correctly. Remember to think about the small details.
- Now write the same conversation but put it on stage and include stage directions. Remember to think about what we will see on the stage.
- Now write the same dialogue as if it were in a short film. Remember to think about what we will see on the screen.
- Use the voices in your dialogue to kickstart a poem.
- Interview two people and write a nonfiction story or a blog post.

Grammarly can help you to punctuate dialogue correctly: https://www.grammarly.com/blog/quotation-marks-and-dialogue/

The BBC Writers' Room contains plenty of resources for writers, including information on how to layout a stage play. http://www.bbc.co.uk/writers

Dialogue: design your own

Spend a day listening to how people speak. You know the drill now: either carry your notebook around and jot down the interesting phrases you hear or write down what sticks in your head at the end of the day. You can do this while going about your everyday business, or go to places to listen to the way people speak – cafés, trains and buses are good as I've said.

See if you can match an emotion (or changing

emotions) to the lines of dialogue you note down. You might also want to make a note of tone of voice. You're only after one or two choice phrases. Don't try to transcribe conversations. Remember: be subtle and stay safe while you do this!

Make a spark box that is only for lines of overheard dialogue. Add to it regularly. When you need an idea for a piece of writing, take out a couple of lines of dialogue and use them to get you started.

8

DIY writing prompts

Using your own writing prompts

There are tips in each section for inventing your own writing prompts, using 'what if?', inventing 'writing rules', creating spark boxes, and combining observations to make something new. Perhaps you've waited until now to come up with them, if so, go back and work through the 'design your own' section of each chapter.

Design a writing schedule. Put in fifteen to thirty-minute slots (regular, by not necessarily every day) for the next month. Allocate some of the writing prompts you have designed yourself to each session.

Here's how to collect together even more writing prompts to use:

- Find online prompts on social media, for example.
- Make your own scrapbook: a physical one, or a virtual one on Pinterest or in Evernote, for example. Collect postcards, images, ephemera,

objects from nature, anything you think could kick off a piece of writing.

- Get hold of *Find Time to Write*, which contains lots more writing prompts. There's more information here: www.louiseton-deur.co.uk/find-time-to-write-time-management-for-writers
- When you turn up in your space to write, begin with one of these writing prompts.

If you've enjoyed this book, please consider leaving a review.

9

Resources

Websites

I've put together a list of websites for writers here: www.louisetondeur.co.uk/websites-for-writers

If you're in the UK, this is a good list of organisations for writers: https://www.writerscentrenorwich.org.uk/support-for-writers/literature-organisations/

You'll find my writing courses linked from here, plus other ways to work with me: www.louisetondeur.co.uk

Books I've mentioned

Adams, Douglas. *The Ultimate Hitchhikers Guide: Five Complete Novels and One Story*. Gramercy Books, 2005.

Austen, Jane. *Pride and Prejudice*. Oxford University Press, 2008.

Beckett, Samuel. *Endgame: A Play in One Act*. Faber & Faber, 2006.

Brontë Charlotte. *Jane Eyre*. Macmillan Heinemann, 2005.

Cron, Lisa. *Story Genius*. Ten Speed Press, 2016.

Doyle, Arthur Conan. *The Adventures of Sherlock Holmes*. Scholastic, 2003.

Elbow, Peter. *Writing with Power: Techniques for Mastering the Writing Process*. Oxford University Press, 1998.

James, Henry. *The Turn of the Screw*. St. Martin's Press, 1995.

Novakovich, Josip. *The Fiction Writer's Workshop*. Writers' Digest Books, 2008.

Shakespeare, William. *Twelfth Night*. Arden Shakespeare, 2008.

Sheridan, Richard. *The Rivals*. Longman, 1985.

Stanislavski, Konstantin. *An Actor Prepares*. Bloomsbury, 2014.

Weiland, K.M. *Structuring Your Novel*. Pen for a Sword, 2013.

About the Author

After doing a Creative Writing MA at The University of East Anglia in the noughties, Lou Tondeur published *The Water's Edge* and *The Haven Home for Delinquent Girls* with Headline Review, did a PhD, travelled around the world, started a family, and became a Creative Writing lecturer. Since then she has supported countless numbers of writers through mentoring and editorial feedback. *Unusual Places*, her first short story collection, came out in 2018, and she is currently working on her next novel. Lou lives near Brighton on the sometimes sunny south coast of England, teaches for the Open University, and blogs at: www.louise tondeur.co.uk

facebook.com/louisetondeurwriter

x.com/LouiseTondeur

instagram.com/louisetondeur

bookbub.com/profile/louise-tondeur

Also by Louise Tondeur

The Small Steps Guide to Goal Setting and Time Management

Find Time to Write

How to Think Like a Writer

How to Write a Novel and Get It Published

Printed in Great Britain
by Amazon